also by Janaka Stucky

The Truth Is We Are Perfect (2015)

The World Will Deny It For You (2012)

Your Name Is The Only Freedom (2009)

ASCEND ASCEND
by Janaka Stucky

THIRD MAN BOOKS
NASHVILLE, TENNESSEE

For more information:
Third Man Books, LLC, 623 7th Ave S, Nashville, Tennessee 37203.

A CIP record is on file with the Library of Congress.

FIRST EDITION

Cover illustration & lettering by Aaron Horkey
Sigils by K Lenore Siner

For music and more information:
http://thirdmanbooks.com/ascendascend
password: silence

ISBN 978-0-9974578-3-4

The author is deeply grateful to Star & Snake for giving him the space within which to do his work.

for Eli

Table of Contents

I heard the noise of their wings, like the noise of many waters, like the voice of the Almighty, a tumult like the noise of an army; and when they stood still, they let down their wings.

— from Ezekiel's vision

FOREWORD

I was standing on a shaded slope of Minnesota woodland the first time I encountered this mystic feast of a poem. Coming from above was the frenzied cry of birds, fighting or fornicating I couldn't tell which. Beneath me was the now-horizontal trunk of a very tall tree, which had cracked over in a recent storm. There was a stream murmuring before me, and behind me a glimpse of one of the many lakeside mansions that seem to loom out of the wilderness more and more often with each passing year. It seemed a very apt spot to get lost in Janaka Stucky's skein of wonder-words about searching for transcendence in the Anthropocene, or, as he puts it "...responding / With purity to the collapsing / Sigh of the world." Incantatory and mesmeric, like all of his poetry, *Ascend Ascend* is a work that begs to be read out loud. And so that is what I did. Pretty soon, I was sighing, too.

I started on my feet, trying to channel the spirit of one of Stucky's shamanic recitations (which if you haven't witnessed yet yourself in person, you must remedy posthaste). As I read, I imagined I was calling up and out, to the birds, to the leaves, to whatever lesser gods of the woods were listening that day. At points my voice would tire, or my knee would give a twinge, and I would sit down on the trunk for a bit, and read more quietly, thinking of bones and stones and roots. Then I'd stand again and read loudly again, shifting from foot to foot. So it went for over an hour, back and forth, back and forth. It struck me as a sort of davening, this up and down motion, the sway. And I thought about how rapturous poetry like Stucky's is so very similar to prayer, for both are embodied entities as much as they are spirit-stuff. They are offerings from the flesh to invisible forces. Tributes from a Me to a Thou. Language is a bridge between realms, then.

And in this work, Stucky proves once again to be a particularly remarkable architect. For, despite its lofty title, his is an intricate and multi-directional construction—as grimy as it is glittering. He shows us that the path of ascension is never a straight line, but rather a circuit of elemental processes we cycle through. We burrow, we fly, we drown, and we burn. We fall before we rise. And so it goes, these great deaths and merciful (re)births happening within and around us every moment of our lives.

He also reminds us that the way to reach the ethereal is by going through the material, with all of its sensual terrors. Where Whitman sang the body electric, Stucky sings "the body exquisite," and with this ode to mud and blood and fungus of all forms, we know he means his own and the heavenly body of Earth, both. These are dwelling places, and as such they are spaces of sublime pleasure and pain—or as Ginsberg wrote, "Holy! Ours! bodies! suffering! magnanimity!" According to Stucky, these bodies house landscapes of

diamonds and excrement, of "the numinous /
Spell of flowers" and "a brilliant storm of
intestines." These bodies are dark and rotting and
full of sweet, holy fire. These bodies are where we
live, and what we'll leave behind.

These sites are sacred not only in their physicality,
however. Our homes hold something more. Some
might call it soul, or quintessence, or maybe even
magic. In Stucky's telling, every layer of the universe
is laced with divinity, as is every moment: "There
is a precise instant when the world / Is marvelous
/ Now / Is its name." In his occult topography,
there are seven heavens amongst the soil, and the
bottom of the sea is equally stuffed with angels and
crustaceans. Here, the seraphic palaces of Merkabah
literature aren't only in the celestial sphere, but are
mapped onto this very planet, rendering it a sort
of supernal terrestrial palimpsest. This work is
an exploration of immanence, as much as it is an
attempt to reach beyond.

And so, *Ascend Ascend* is a poem about beingness. It
reflects the perpetual ricochet between poles that
all organic creatures experience, but which human
consciousness renders all the more gorgeous, and
all the more ghastly. We're led through earth, air,
water, and fire. We shimmy up the Tree of Life,
get caught in its labyrinth of limbs, and tumble
back down again. Stucky's lines show us that the
Kabbalistic sefirot are footholds that can launch
us into higher consciousness, or trip us up entirely,
and that so often the greatest discoveries occur

along the route from one position to the next. It's a treacherous ordeal, this eternal transmutation from one condition to another. Sacred and profane; spiritual and corporeal; exhilarated and excruciated; As Above, So Below: the tension between these states constantly threatens to obliterate us. But Stucky's piece asks the question: what if obliteration is the point?

For who hasn't longed, on some fleeting occasions at least, to let go of oneself entirely? To merge with the grand Whatever It Is that makes this world so difficult and bright? Certainly the ecstatic poets that Stucky is a successor of all express this very sentiment. One can't help but think of the "ancestors of ancestors speaking with centuries / Upon centuries of mouths" with whom he is in dialogue: Hafiz, Blake, Yeats, Doolittle, and di Prima, to name but a few. So often, their poems are about surrendering to some sanctified source, and then melting away into it. Rumi wrote "Let the caller and the called disappear; be lost in the Call." And per Kabir: "I'll keep uttering / The name / And lose myself / In it."

But rather than give over to its thrall, poets instead take on the impossible task of trying to pin the wings of the ineffable with words. In doing so, they grant the reader a bit of flight as well.

Ascend Ascend touches upon this paradox, for it is also a poem about language. Alphabets, intonations, and supernatural syllables are referenced throughout the work. Stucky is engaging in "adamic / Choreography," putting names to things with the elated mania of first man. I thought about this, too, as I finished reading it to the woods, and then found myself looking around stupefied. Adam's own name comes from adamah, meaning "earth," and in stringing the world with words, he created it anew, before being swallowed up by it once more.

Stucky's writing is a miracle, not only in its genius, but in its generosity. This is a love poem that shocks with secret links and revelations. It will let you forget yourself if you allow it to, for this is "a blade / Of light cutting / The umbilical cord of I." It will lift you out of whoever you think you are.

When it's done, you'll come back to the body where you began, a bit dirtier and more devoted than before.

Pam Grossman
author of *Waking the Witch:*
Reflections on Women, Magic, and Power

Blessed is the lotus
The day's bleeding wound

Blessed are the spiders their alphabet
Twenty six stones my corpse is dancing

Blessed are the worms the maggots
Sexless and probing like tongues

Through the rotting soil

Blessed is the loam

Blessed is the loam the darkness
Mushrooms blooming teeth pushing

Through the earth's black and putrid gums

Blessed is the Maw
The Great Maw the mouth the gnashing
Of continental shores

Blessed are the stones the rocks
The island all the world a promontory scab
Hardening around the earth's myriad
Molten wounds

Blessed is the blood the bile ascending
The gross moss of shapeless years forming

On the eyeless trunks of trees

Blessed are the snakes the dragons
Breathing the giants eating each dumb
Beast our mothers our fathers filled with blood

Blessed are the black cricket's legs singing
Furiously until the whole lake is on fire

Blessed is the fire
Blessed is the lake
Blessed are the cricket's black legs

Blessed is the trembling nerve of now
The great topaz hurtling through
Galactic dark

Blessed is the dark the knotted roots
Of the first tree the fearful serpent
Uncoiling still as even the first
Stone turns to dust

Blessed is our fear
The Great Retching which rips us
Wide-eyed hairy and blood spattered
Terribly laughing up from the mud

Blessed is the transfiguration of terror that wakens
The crimson thread within

Blessed is our weaving and braiding
Our crawling

Blessed is our climb

Blessed are we who flop from mud
To soil to grass to trees

Blessed are our lungs our hands

Blessed is the transmutation of air
And fruit and meat to spirit

Blessed are the bees
Blessed is their hive returning

Through each flaw of rain revealing
The heirophany of nectar
In the fresh light of the cloud's empty womb

Blessed is our moaning and shitting
Our walking on quivering feet

Blessed is our walking and running
Our speaking each day our dying

Our struggle toward freedom our dying
Blessed is the fight for freedom
Even more than to be free

Blessed is our life
Blessed is our instrument responding
With purity to the collapsing
Sigh of the world

Blessed is our cry
Our cry our radiant repeating

The gleaming cinder

Like honey like wax like roses
The world vanishing and nothing
But us remaining beneath the abyss
Of god singing

I am the one that is not

And when the cry comes to no longer
Be the vessel the cry comes
Not from your mouth
Alone it is not you talking

It is ancestors of ancestors speaking with centuries
Upon centuries of mouths it is
Not you alone desiring it is

A galaxy of descendants desiring
Down the long fathomless
Pillar of your infinite heart

For between the void and the abyss
You alone struggle and are imperiled

And in your small earthen chest
One thing alone struggles and is imperiled

And when the cry comes
The cry comes in the cryptic tongue

To pass beyond my body bastion
Of sugar and bone

My body
Monstrously shining above
Black lichen rivers

Its curse like a star of blood erupting
From my throat

A promise roaring
Jackals howling
Awful and grim

My body my body
Lust magnificent
Views of Byzantium
Crucified awake in me
In me among

My body idle and brutal
Let light thunder
The first to adore

My body my ghost
My retinue of ghouls

Profane and dancing
Dizzy drunk and shrieking
Through a phantasmagoria of stars

My body exquisite
Thighs streaming with blood

My body hungry and gaping
Threaded with hands

My body my tongue distended
And dangling amid corpses
And noncorpses
Gungung drone the bees

My body my mouth
My penetrated mouth singing
Through the honeycomb locked in its jaws

My penetrated body
Levitating weightless
Rotted by this leprous alien song

I am penetrated
I am penetrated
I am pierced

My body my elephant my chariot
I am pierced

I am penetrated by men

I am penetrated by insects plants and beasts
The ecstatic march of flesh

I am penetrated by birds by stones
And the wind's twisted shell

I am penetrated by seas and fires
By colors by wings
By horns by claws

By constellations
Butterflies

I am penetrated
By great hemlocks blackening
The moonless sky
I am penetrated

By water by dreams
By lightning cracks in mute night

By night by night thick as death
It must be death

I am penetrated by death and cannot see

And beneath the night sky the universe
Of every eye judging acutely
With their small fires

Igniting to the orchard within
Me the path of names

Every word along the way
Lit like a flame upon
The wick of its origin

I kiss each name and make
For it a temple on my tongue I name

A stone I name an insect I name
An idea dancing across
A dust mote's horizonless stage

I name a nightmare
Ecstasy

I name sleep
A fertile wall of storms

I name the air choked
With a blizzard of blossoms
White origin of apples
Buzzing on the wild threadless sun

I name the eye of the earth blinking in my blood
A phenomena of swarms

I name the hour black lightning
And its children golden sheaves of fire
Burning Lanka to the ground

I name this fever a flood like
A harras of feral horses breaking
On the blackened plain

And the trembling shale of stardust is its name
Red java flower is its name

The sky lit by heaping nectar
Is its name

The cloud whose throne is a corpse
Is its name

Dwell in its presence in dread
Is its name

Reflect on the root from which you were hewn
Is its name

An act without knowledge is nothing
Is its name

The seven heavens of chaos
Is its name

Vilon is its name
Raki'a is its name
Shehakim is its name
Zevul is its name
Ma'on is its name
Makhun is its name
Aravot is its name

A curtain like the hum of a severed head
Is its name

The firmament scattered like a riddle
Is its name

The millstone grinding bright miracle of wheat
Is its name

A silver bridge of the dead returning
To their infinite numinous source
Is its name

A choir of thousands terrifying slow and rising
From a single mouth is its name

Scorched by the awestruck jism of a new element
Is its name

Amen amen nezah selah is its name

There is a precise instant when the world
Is marvelous

Now
Is its name

I hear its cry

I hear its cry
Lacerated by a paradise of sadness

Devoured by brutes

I hear its cry
Ashen with the incandescent
Dust of rubies

I hear its cry I rise
Weeping

A moth emerging
From the innocence of limbo
Beneath the green bowers

I hear its cry
Dissolving in a golden beam

I invent new beasts
New flowers new stars
New men new holes
Pool of Bethesda
New flesh new tongues
New purity O purity
This vision of purity
Erect for the brief bliss of the void

With their pestilential breath abating
I leave the hazel copse

I depart through nameless
Numberless years

Climb the cosmic mountain
Parapets of jasper shining
Above the waning cypress
Wading through thickets of mallow
I approach the navel of the earth

From the trunk of a gum tree
I fashion the sacred pole

Anoint it and climb
Belligerently ascend
And climb
Further still
I climb
And disappear
Into the sky

I exchange the world for this
Strange thing which is flight

And though I flee none pursue

For reasons stronger than the provision of law
I ascend with agony

For reasons inherent in tears in grief
In death in blood
In gestures in objects

I ascend with agony

For reasons inherent
In matter itself
I ascend with agony

I ascend a trembling
Phosphorescence dragging itself upwards into
The immense blue of every distant dawn

I ascend with agony
And watch the tremulous Invisible
By way of crowning horror tread

On all living things ascending
Ascending I ascend

I am the name itself

The is itself I am
The limit of the great dream

The secret immediate movement
From which the milk of our unknowing
Pours forth

I unbind
In the slow feint of the Invisible
And have only the order of my breath

The liturgy of dissonant swarms
Ascend ascend

Here where the ravenous
Mane of devotion is whispered
In each worshipful beating

I ascend

I ascend with agony the music
Of great abandonment blossoming in
The decay of which I am assured

I ascend with agony a center
Of luminous vapor shedding

Its garments of malediction
The gravity of this re-turn

I ascend with agony to conquer
The temptation of hope

Free from the terror of my seeking heart
I ascend

I ascend with agony above
The inexhaustible graveyard of the earth
I ascend with agony

My unextinguished
Body blackening like a thistle
At the edge of its radiant limbs

I ascend with agony amid fetid groans echoing
The nausea of sobbing fruits

I ascend I ascend

I ascend
With agony debauched and suffocating
In the voice of my own destruction ascend

I ascend with agony vibrating
In the stillness of every orphaned hand

I ascend with agony mutilated
By sadness at the world's eclipsing I

I ascend with agony this wagon of dying
Each wheel driven through hordes by the invisible whip
I ascend
I ascend

I ascend

With agony drowning in the corpse of vinegar
Honey and milk dripping
From the lion's flesh
The ox and eagle drinking
The bestial tides of heaven

I ascend with agony misery shimmering
From fingertip to toe in the moldering
Wind of my existence ascending
I ascend

I ascend with agony from the chestnut of sorrow

The beautiful communal name
Of the breath that will wreck you
On the bank of millioned bodies writhing
Through a brilliant storm of intestines
The shimmering ulcer of fuck

I ascend with agony and psalm
The black honey of my circumcision

I ascend with agony through milky smoke of cypress
Burning

A flaming bed for the counterfeit of moonlit night

Ascend I ascend

I ascend with agony a diamond forming
Like tears drying
In ten-thousand-year-old
Excrement of the dead

I ascend with agony the gleaming rib
Of an angel spinning in silent adoration

For the dusk beyond the white gate
I ascend

With agony I ascend
A sepulcher companionless

My empty skull soundlessly
Drunk on the laughter of tears

I ascend with agony devouring
The ashes of my waking

The black river of solitude glorified

Amphibian hunger of our legion decadent spleen

I ascend with agony a wingless sword
Anointed in the violet pus of stars

I ascend with agony embroidered
To the alphabet of a ceaseless jasmine sun

I ascend with agony hardening like wax
In the absent dream of fire

With agony I ascend I ascend
With agony the agony the poverty
Of a scythe that drives its saying
Across the century's lilac face

I ascend with agony and write
My affliction in the homesick
Ravines of my terrifying hand

I ascend with agony my mouth open
Above the world a vapor of blood

I ascend lamenting like grass blades
Over each syllable of hell buried
In the marvelous wine of the earth

I ascend
Chalk
Dust
And sunlight

I ascend
Effluvium of despair

I ascend
A stygian tide of black flies

Carcassing the wind
I ascend

I ascend with agony the city of my torso
Tattered by the numinous
Spell of flowers

Knives and beating wings

I ascend with agony
Ascending

A sunflower weapon
Blinking in the butchered glorious hum

I ascend with agony the music of rotting
Apples chafing my scented skull

I ascend with agony caparisoned by poppies
By black stars and the shivering
Tissue of vice

I ascend with agony
Drinking fever
Drinking storms
My storms
Drinking storms
I ascend

Into the sky like a bronze gate
I ascend

Sky like a roofless church
With birds of flame
Perched along its rim I ascend

Sky like great teeth of the sea
Rabid with lilacs of foam I ascend

Sky like a blade
Of light cutting
The umbilical cord of I I ascend

Sky like primordial honey
I ascend

Sky like mellifluous rot
I ascend

Sky like a garden
Dug with the white edge of a scream I ascend

Sky my dark wings beating
The fountain the flood
That comes before the abyss

I ascend

I ascend
My sky my hour my night
My gleaming needle haloed ascending

I ascend

Sky like the death of juniper
Quivering in the clitoral spell of sleep

Sky that wakes like acacias
Blind from the cradled soil

Sky like a great and boundless longing
Setting fire to itself ascending

I ascend
I ascend

I ascend with agony a blackbird egg
Hatching in the alcove of a lion's jaw

I ascend with agony devoured and spiraling
Upwards into countless crowns

I ascend with agony summoning
A plague of flowers white blood swirling

From their indestructible glistening
Cheeks I ascend

I ascend with agony lifted alone
By the memory of milk I ascend

I ascend with agony my guillotine
Of laughter raised high above
The neck of the wind ascending
I ascend

I ascend through an omega
Of astonishment

I ascend with agony carved from the wind by
The knife that bears my sign

I ascend with agony
In the solstice of humiliation

I shall love
I shall love
I shall love

I ascend in the bright flame of marigolds

I shall love
I shall love

I ascend

The sea hovers above you
As you soundlessly drown upward in the
Fathomless ceiling of kingless generations

Astounded and perfect
In the higher octave of self

You
The enlightened person of blood

In the knotted finger of a leper
I am hidden and
I am not

O celestial city
Created before the city
Was built by the human hand

The form delineated from distant
Ages by the writing of the Heaven of Stars

I dream I do not exist

And in my dream of me I dream
I am a mist of birds
Upon a drop of insect blood

A great flight of violence
A glass ship shattering
In the nationless flood

A mongrel grave swarming
With flowers in acrid azalean gloom

And to the candle I give a spear
To the morning star a body of hemp
To abiding shame an ax
To the expected guest an oak tree
To the house the cemetery of the world around it
To my coffin an apple
Shining in the atramentous night

Thus with my piceous abdomen bloated
By the sweet gift of rot I descend
Through impenetrable cobalt depths

Flickering down through submarine trenches
My vigil long as the path of a flame

Emerging from profane duration
To recover unmoving time
I explode in blood sublimely to return to the larval
Modality of existence

I explode in blood sublimely to descend
My shadow past the tablet
Upon which is written
The names of beneficent stars

I explode in blood sublimely past jellyfish
Throbbing blind and endless in their appetite

I explode in blood sublimely here
Inside the great dream
Of a carnivorous whale

I explode in blood sublimely I
The child of matter perish and build
My dwelling as I descend

Into the resined black sphere of
A crab's enormous eye

I explode in blood sublimely
Rags of light honeycomb my emerald dying

I explode in blood sublimely spindle
Down through a jade of tears

I explode in blood sublimely free
From the terror of my seeking heart

Knives ripening the pith of salt

Urchin wool icebergs and the succor of starfish
Cruel harvest of orgies threshing
Carnations from the glass cage of doves

I explode in blood sublimely the water
All around spelling my name
In the iris of each dazzling halo

I explode in blood sublimely
The night of my blood like wild cherries
Staining the lips of leviathan angels

I explode in blood sublimely sexlessly
Descending through the quaking

Unchangeable aeon of eyelashes
Forever closing beneath the weight of dawn

I explode in blood sublimely
Perform signs and wonders for the
Forty nine indestructible demons

Until their amazement splits in two
Their unshakable dread

I explode in blood sublimely
Extinguish in chasms my neptune violence

And echo
And echo
The labyrinth of our heart's thundering conch

I explode in blood sublimely
Stardust bleeding
Through a thousand thousand years
Into this rainbowed sex of light
The world called my body

Now answering perpetually outward
Over infinite hours like the blink
A diamond makes when it wakes

From intransient slumber
I explode in blood sublimely
Stubbornly surviving the miraculous
Sine wave of bangs

Falling unsure as planets
From the radiant black spear

I explode in blood sublimely my blood
A hymn a choral canticle of dying

Which sings beyond all thought
Until I reach the pit

I explode in blood sublimely adorning
The abandoned daturas of seraphim

Their androgynous burning
Beneath one million tons of sea water
In an ancient canyon igniting
With silence and spectral sheen

I explode in blood sublimely
The dove colored skree of oblivion
Descending

Denser and denser
Still denser

Descending

Until I breach the ocean's
Swarming floor

And I am the crown of strangers
Dripping ragged rows of teeth
Dripping dabberlocks of kelp

The sightless hunger fanging
Endlessly into hollow depths

I am the preworld objectless scape of ink

Extolling the deathbell forever
Calling each fin to sup

I am the eater of history and darkness

Fattening my teeth
On the wild misery of knives

I am the root of the tongue

Bit off to guard against
The benthic memory of death

I am the ambush of prophecy
Illuminating the abyssal plain

Formless
Fathomless insomnia of stars
Through which angels unendingly dream
Of filling their ever widening mouths
With the wet muscles of
Infinite human dead

I explode in blood sublimely
Each epoch of my red milk
Forged to tendrils of perfect knowing
In the ceaseless gentle hammering of gills

Here where the worthless
Rings of history mime the world's hunger

Here where the translucent fruit of sleep
Capsizes to shadowless nothing

Here where tentacles clench unclench and grasp
The haunted crystalline tomorrows
Of our stale and venomous moans

Here where disbanded heavens
Noon the breathing oath
The leavetaking of our senses
Senselessly measured now

Here where drowning plants the first
Kiss of remembering upon
The ecstatic lamentation of our descent

I explode in blood sublimely
Dispossessed approaching the negative
Dusk of rainbows extinguished
In the belly of a terrible worm

I explode in blood sublimely consumed
By the surging tide smiling wide
Smiling wide
Soothed in the gore of my undoing
Ever widening
Smiling wide

I explode in blood sublimely
Flushed with fevers dreaming
Down strangling and twined
Forever strangling in the seagrass
Twining judgement of the flesh

I explode in blood sublimely
The darkness receive me
The water receive me

The infinite sea of my heart receive me

The angels receive me
Amid their thrashing enormous flippers
And fins receive me

Amid the thunderous gnashing of
Their unutterable teeth receive me

Amid their cavernous and holy
Gullets receive me

Amid great unwinding threshing
Tentacles of their tongues receive me

Amid the flood of the numinous
Bile receive me

Amid the spectacular mystery
Of their vengeance receive me

Amid the heaviest night of fallen
Atrocity receive me

Amid the sanctuary of their horror
Their ancient celestine appetite receive me

Amid their glutted
Cosmic uncoiling
Receive me
Receive me

Amid their sick and ravenous crowns
Receive me

Their savage annunciation of gore
Receive me

Gargantuan craws thrumming with ichor
Receive me
Receive me

Receive me
Receive me

I explode in blood sublimely
Seething multitudes over
Sunken mountains
Primordial and boundless

Bloomed in dilating seraphic veins
I explode in blood sublimely
Transparent and eyeless
Bristlemouthed and angling

Groping the hadopalegic darkness
In bony dimorphic dread

I explode in blood sublimely
Fragmented

As I am
In the moment so fragile

Free from the spell
Of the word and its shadow

I reach to seize
The is of nothing

The fourth dimension of the eternal

Now
And like

An insect I buzz
Hallelujah into the abyss

In the absence of stars
No light no word no thing
No memory of name

You hear only voices

Laughter and weeping

The fluttering of wings

I unfold in the now of nonbeing

The thorn of the first letter

Bonfire of the invisible
Nucleus of purity
In which I contort and blaze

Fire is the first and final mask

The mystery grown savage

Dread essence beyond logic
Weeping from the pyre

Here every word
Every letter is an ark
Within which I shudder divining
The Great Shame to be
Its dreadful core

And if I say I am shattered by an erotic wind

And if I say I am consumed by a colossal dread

Impossible mouth
Ringed with blood and tears

I approach the Great Shame

I draw ever near
The Great Shame which continues incessantly

The Great Shame from which there is no return

The Great Shame in which I establish
The ecstasy that can never be established
In words but which I struggle
Unceasingly to establish in words

The Great Shame who is deathless I collaborate
With and become immortal

The Great Shame behind
Whose ceaseless flux I discern
Indestructible unity

The Great Shame the law
Of our bodies breaking
Both theory and practice
Ashes and nothing
Beyond which nothing exists

The Great Shame on every
Face the same mask
We burn against the same dark
In the same

Hour which is now

The Great Shame possessing
Neither victory nor vertigo

The Great Shame spectating
Above the abyss

The Great Shame working
In sleep abominable
Marvelously renouncing
The order of hope

This is our name Great Shame transmuting
The heart's bright humiliation
Into a ceaselessly expanding joy

This is our great name eternal
Palaces of the dead

This is our great name
Ashes and nothing
The nothing beyond
Perfection of nothing
Ashes and nothing
The infinite possibility of dread

This is our great name
The flower our error
The seed of our speaking
In the terror of the This of Now

This is our great name
The salvation of the mirror
Perfectly empty
Ashes and nothing
The unqualified wholeness of being

This is our great name
The patient brutality of sweetness
Ashes and nothing
Orgasmic apocalypse
Dismantling the ellipses longing to cease

This is our great name
Ashes and nothing
The great prerogative of beauty subduing
The durable fire
The sea

Ashes and nothing
The transport of joy revealing
Of which we cannot speak

Ashes and nothing
The spark of a torch in darkness

The Great Signified burning
And turning to ashes and nothing
The dissonant alphabetic throng

A fire soaking wings

This is our great name
Plucked quill from an angel etching
Ashes and nothing
Each black letter in the twenty two names
I create for god

Ashes and nothing
Awake and singing
Cleave to me
Supernal Mystery of Dust

Ashes and nothing
Awake and singing
Cleave to me
The Shadow Called the Field of Blood

Awake and singing
Cleave to me
The Seventh Note of a Dark Tree
Humming in the Wind

Cleave to me
O Aria of tangled intestines
Suffering through tears of milk

Cleave to me
Crusade of phantoms striking
Amber through the cyprian clouds

Cleave to me
Newborn white smile
In a grim dungeon of heartbeats

Cleave to me
Geography of Legends

Cleave to me
Constant Uncertainty of Outcomes

Cleave to me
Adobe of premonition

Cleave to me
Torch of mathematics kindling
The planet's next position

Cleave to me my dream of waking
From the Dream of Waking

Cleave to me
O Low Enjoying Power

Cleave to me blushing
Ledge of human eye

Cleave to me adamic
Choreography of empyrean locust drone

Cleave to me comet
Uncalled ecstasy plunging
Seventy two measures into the abyss

Cleave to me thy bright grip
On a lancet revealing
Our heart's vivid shame

Cleave to me anthracite
Insomnia awake
For millennia waiting to burn

Cleave to me first star
O arsonous pyre
We place hope upon
Beyond our geriatric reach

Cleave to me pith of zero
White maggot pulsing in the emerald grass

Cleave to me great grime of camphor
Skirmishing our lungs

Cleave to me sodomite dream
Of cromlechs miraculous among the coral trees

Cleave to me
Grey limbs of lava
Embracing in ruin

Cleave to me great name
This is your name
Free from the amen loosening
Its hair on the chasm of my tongue

Free from the om
The shanti rising
In a vultured gaping gold

Free from the Adonai Elohim
El
Eloah
Shadai
Ehyah
Tsevoat

Free from Alumdulilah burning
La ilaha illa Allah
La ilaha illa
Hu

Free from Namah Shivaya
Jah

Tet-vav Hossanah Baha
Without beginning or end
Ashes and nothing
Ameen Amen

And free from the name I dwell
In the star-ringed arnica of great listening
Larded with orchids
And the ashlar odor of light

I am the breath
Crouching in the soft refusal of ever

Transfiguring fire to dew

I am the stone which is not a stone
The contraction of two embraces
The mutation of So into I

I am

The intolerable suffering
The leaping reef of suns
Heartblood pouring from a ram horn
On the pubic shadow of the earth

I am the thick smoke of scorpions
A Seder dismantling tomorrow upon
My fingers
My murdered looms

I am the Great Absence
Scandal of astonishment

Icelight of gallowed sky naked
Bathing in the Is of This

I am the noose of every vowel descending
From the hidden face of ŌŌŌŌŌ

I am the aurora of ovum
Whose green duration
Writes the synonym of the world

Through one quarter of one hundred
Thousand years I am

The hymn of hysteria placed within
Each star's ruptured infernal mouth

I am the Silence composed of eternal present
Indefinitely recoverable

Silence where even
The noise of nothing does not exist

Silence great pearl of Silence

The skin with which the fire first touches the Void

The Yes of silence
Formed by a Yuga of No

And in the silence

The silence
Of silence

The phenomena of swarms
Singing

I am the one that is not

Through the lotus of the day's bleeding wound

Key to the Seven Archangelic Seals

SIGIL   RESONANCES

 Uriel (Enoch) / Mikael (Testament of Solomon) / Michael (Gnostics) :: Elemental resonance with Earth. Invoked within to dwell in Assiah, the Material World.

 Raphael (Enoch) / Gabriel (Testament of Solomon) / Gabriel (Gnostics) :: Elemental resonance with Air. Invoked within to dwell in Yetzirah, the World of Formation.

 Zerachial (Enoch) / Arael (Testament of Solomon) / Barachiel (Gnostics) :: Invoked within to traverse Samekh [Mem], the path between Yesod (Foundation), Hod (Splendor), and Netzach (Victory).

 Raguel (Enoch) / Uriel (Testament of Solomon) / Raphael (Gnostics) :: Invoked within to approach Tiphareth, the Beauty [Grace] beyond the Veil.

 Gabriel (Enoch) / Ioath (Testament of Solomon) / Sealtiel (Gnostics) :: Elemental resonance with Water. Invoked within to dwell in Beri'ah, the World of Creation.

 Ramiel (Enoch) / Adonael (Testament of Solomon) / Jehudiel (Gnostics) :: Invoked within to travel Daleth / Gimel and traverse Daath (Knowledge) [the Abyss].

 Michael (Enoch) / Sabrael (Testament of Solomon) / Uriel (Gnostics) :: Elemental resonance with Fire. Invoked within to dwell in Atziluth, the Archetypal World.

Photo by Adrianne Mathiowetz

Janaka Stucky is the publisher and founding editor
of Black Ocean. He lives with his wife and son
in Massachusetts, where he cultivates a sense of
possibility and other forms of radical worship.